Clever Costumes

BY SHANNON WHITT
PHOTOGRAPHS BY E. H. WALLOP

downtown bookworks

downtown 🏙 bookworks

With love and gratitude to my mom, Becky Whitt, for all her clever costumes! And to Kieran and Jonah for all their help!

XO,
Shannon

A big THANK YOU to our models: Bethanycordelia Chin, Sanaeda Halyard, Emma Hannan, Dexter Magratten, Grace Osborne, Gabriela Perez, Paula Perez, Jaelen Pinkney, Jonah Smith, Kieran Smith, Avery St. Clair, Roshi Soans, Carolina Thomas, and Mariana Thomas.

Design by Georgia Rucker Design
How-to illustrations: Georgia Rucker
All photography: E. H. Wallop
Typeset in Paris, Museo, and Retrozoid

Crafty Pants series
Copyright © 2013 Downtown Bookworks Inc.
All rights reserved.

Printed in China
April 2013

ISBN 13-9781935703310

10 9 8 7 6 5 4 3 2 1

Downtown Bookworks Inc.
285 West Broadway
New York, NY 10013

www.dtbwpub.com

All kit materials conform to CPSC standards.

NOTE: With any craft project, check product labels to make sure that the materials you use are safe and nontoxic. The instructions in this book are intended to be followed with adult supervision.

CONTENTS

BASIC INSTRUCTIONS

TRANSFORM YOURSELF!

IT'S SO MUCH BETTER THAN STORE-BOUGHT!

Using the contents of this kit plus stuff from around the house, *Clever Costumes* shows you how to turn yourself into an eye-popping alien, a chicken, a pirate, or a princess, to name a few possibilities—and it's all super easy! Once you get the hang of things, let your imagination run wild!

There are photographs of each finished costume, along with easy-to-follow general instructions. Even younger kids will be able to tackle many of these projects with minimal help from a grown-up.

ROAD-TESTED TIPS

MEASURING ELASTIC Wrap elastic around your waist without stretching it, so that it feels snug but not tight; add 3 to 4 inches for tying the ends.

CUTTING SURFACES If you happen to have an actual craft cutting board, use it, especially when fringing plastic bags or doing any cutting with a craft knife—**which you should do only with the help of a grown-up.** If you don't own a craft cutting board, an old kitchen cutting board can work, too.

STICKING DOUBLE-SIDED TAPE There are different types of double-sided tape. Any of them will work with these projects. When working with tape that comes with a peel-off layer, cut the length of tape you need. Stick it down where you want it to go. **Then** peel off the top protective layer covering the second sticky side.

SUPER-EASY STEP-BY-STEPS

On the following 13 pages, you will find instructions for making costume parts for a bunch of different looks in the book. Once you master these, get inspired to add your own twists for a truly unique creation.

MIX AND MATCH

Ideally, the DIY dress-up ideas in this book will inspire you to come up with your own creative costumes using materials you have around the house. You should also feel free to mix and match the looks we've photographed. For example, make the billowy Queen of Hearts skirt in different colors and pair it with a bag vest.

NOTE: The adhesive-backed, re-closeable, fuzzy-fasteners that come with this kit, will be called fasteners in costume instructions.

BAG SKIRT AND HOLE-PUNCH WAISTBAND

This technique is used for the pirate girl, rocker girl, and the Queen of Hearts skirt, as well as for the Queen of Hearts neck ruffle, the princess wrist ruffles, and the fairy ankle ruffles.

1. Find plastic bags with folded expandable sides (gussets) like the ones in the illustration. For a short skirt, use shorter/shallower bags. For a longer skirt, use bigger/deeper bags. To figure out the number, see "How Many Bags?" below.

2. Flatten the bags (tucking in the gussets) and place them on a work surface facing the same direction. Run a strip of double-sided tape down the side of one bag and tape down the next bag so it overlaps the first. Using this method, tape the bags to each other in a row to create a strip of plastic bags. Trim the handles.

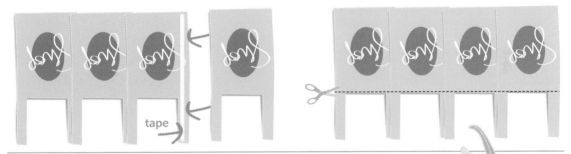

tape

3. Flip over the row of taped-together bags to their wrong side. Run a strip of masking tape across the closed edge. Use a ruler and pencil to mark 1-inch measures along the tape strip. Punch holes at the mark points in the middle of the tape strip.

back of taped-together bags

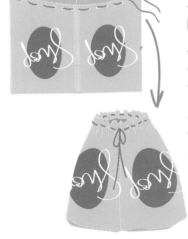

4. Measure a length of elastic cord for your waist (see page 4). Secure a large safety pin to one end of the elastic to keep it from pulling through as you weave it in and out of the holes. Tie off the elastic in a knot. Tape the two open seams of the skirt closed with either double-sided or clear packing tape. Fluff out the gussets and layers.

HOW MANY BAGS? It's not an exact science. A skirt should be poufy when it's drawn in by the elastic cord or pulled in with a ribbon sash. When taping the bags together in a strip (see illustration above), or cutting plastic liners or tablecloths, the width needs to be 2 to 2½ times wider than the circumference of your waist for a short skirt. For the longer skirts, 2 to 3 times wider than the circumference of your waist works better for more pouf and ease in walking.

5

RIBBON SASH SKIRT

This technique is used for the princess, space girl, and mermaid skirts, as well as the ruffle cuffs for the clown. The witch and wolf girl also use this style skirt, with a shredded hem.

1. Run masking tape across the width of the plastic material on its wrong side. Use a ruler and pencil to mark 1-inch measures along the tape strip as shown.

2. Fold the tape in half the long way, as shown. Use scissors to make short cuts at each mark along the strip. (Do not cut all the way through the tape.)

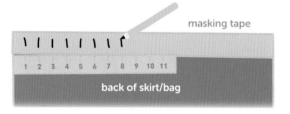

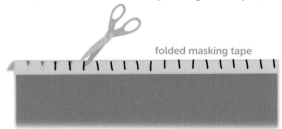

3. Flip the plastic over to its right side; thread ribbon through the slits created by the folded cuts.

4. Wrap the skirt around the waist, tie it closed, and adjust the folds. Cut the hem to desired length, if using liner or tablecloth. If using bags, just fluff.

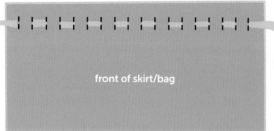

SPACE GIRL NOTE: Use a single sheet of bubble paper that wraps 2 to 2½ times around the circumference of your waist. If you need to tape smaller pieces of bubble paper together to get the right size sheet, use clear packing tape. Also, use clear packing tape instead of masking tape for the strip of tape on the inside top edge of the skirt. Trim the skirt with the blue duct tape that comes with the kit.

PRINCESS NOTE:
To make the long, two-tiered princess skirt, lay a shorter layer of material on top of the longer piece and fasten the pieces by running a strip of double-sided tape across the outside top edge before running the strip of masking tape along the inside top edge.

double-sided tape

front of shorter layer

front of longer layer

masking tape

back of skirt/bags

We show this technique for the bumblebee skirt, but you can use it any time you are using a liner or plastic tablecloth as your skirt material. It's super easy.

EASY ELASTIC-TUNNEL WAISTBAND

1. Cut the plastic to be 2 to 2½ times wider than the circumference of your waist. Run a strip of double-sided tape across width of the plastic on the wrong side.

2 to 2½ times wider than waist measurement

double-sided tape

back of skirt/bag

2. Fold the top over 2 inches and stick down, creating about a ½-inch-deep tunnel.

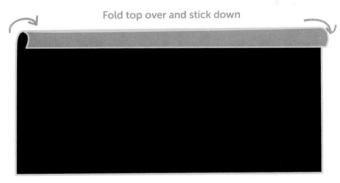

Fold top over and stick down

3. Fasten a safety pin to the end of an elastic cord. Use the safety pin to help you feed the elastic through the tunnel. Knot elastic ends closed and tuck back into the tunnel pocket.

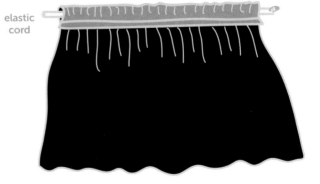

elastic cord

4. Tape the open seams of skirt closed with clear packing tape or double-sided tape.

SIMPLEST VEST

The pirate, hippie, rocker, and witch costumes use these vest techniques. By making variations on the way they are closed or cut, you will give the bag and the fringe vests a different look—laces vs. pins or long fringe vs. shorter fringe.

1. Take an old, adult-size, V-neck T-shirt and cut off the sleeves as shown.

2. Make a cut down the center from the point of the V-neck to the bottom of the shirt. Voilà—a vest!

BAG VEST

1. Flatten a plastic bag on your work surface.

2. Fold it in half and then cut the bottom of the folded bag in a zig-zag pattern.

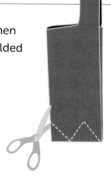

3. Unfold the bag, lift the top layer, and cut directly up the center of that layer.

4. Partially fold open the front sides of the vest and run a strip of masking tape down the inside edges of the vest to reinforce them. Punch holes down each side of the vest. Lace up with ribbon or cord or fasten with really big safety pins.

masking tape

inside of bag vest

FRINGED VEST

1. Cut the collar, sleeves, and button plackets off a button-down shirt and set the pieces aside. Turn the shirt inside out so the pocket doesn't show.

2. Run a piece of tape inside and across the width of the shirt as a stop line for cutting the bottom fringe. Fringe the bottom of the shirt using scissors.

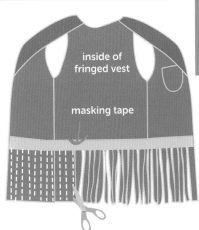

inside of fringed vest

masking tape

3. Flatten one of the sleeves you removed on a cutting surface. If the shirt on hand is long-sleeved, trim the sleeve to a short-sleeved length before cutting fringe. Cut along the under seam and the crease to make two pieces.

Cut along all sewn edges to make two shapes.

4. Tape the straight sleeve edge to a cutting surface and fringe the curved edge of the sleeve as shown. Repeat with the other piece.

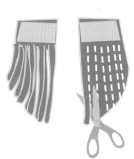

ALTERNATE METHOD
You can do this vest with a V-neck T-shirt for a slightly different, less structured look, which we use on our hippie girl.

5. Glue the sleeve fringe to the shirt-vest with the longer pieces of fringe closest to the open edge of the vest. NOTE: When gluing fringe to vest, protect the inside back of the vest from glue drippings with a few sheets of scrap paper.

tacky glue

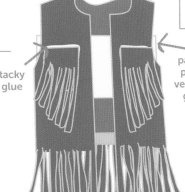

paper to protect vest while gluing

FRINGED POPOVER

CUTTING AND SIZING THE POPOVER BASE

1. The popover base is the bag to which you will attach the fringe layers. Use a large plastic bag that's a bit heavier than the bag you use for fringe. Flatten the base bag you are going to use on your work surface. Trim away the closed bottom, the handles, and one side, as shown. Set the handles aside.

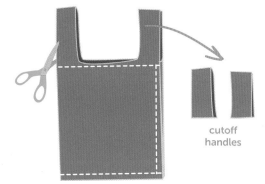

cutoff handles

2. Opened flat, it will look like a longish plastic rectangle. (If you have a plastic tablecloth or shower-curtain liner, you could cut up one of those as a base instead.) Trim the base bag to fit comfortably around your body with an inch or two overlap. Be sure that you will be able to walk and move freely once the fasteners are closed. Run one set of strips down the left-side seam. Run the other set of strips inside and down the right side of the base.

cut-open bag

fastener strips

MAKING FRINGE AND ATTACHING IT TO THE POPOVER

1. Tape the closed end of the bag you're going to fringe to a cutting board or knife-proof surface and cut away the open end.

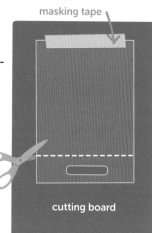

masking tape

cutting board

2. Use a craft knife and a ruler to fringe the entire width of the bag,* as shown. This makes one fringe strip.

Must have a grown-up do this for you.

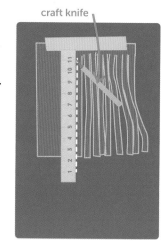

craft knife

10

3. Repeat step 2 for as many fringe strips as you determine you need to cover the popover. There is no correct number. It depends upon the size of the popover, how fringy you want it to look and whether you plan to cover the whole thing.

4. Open the popover base and lay it flat on the work surface. You are ready to add fringe layers.

5. Starting at the bottom and using clear packing tape, attach the fringe strips to the popover. If you like, do the back and sides as well as the front for a full-on fringy alien!

6. If using white bubble paper (from mailer bags) for straps, cut them out and staple them to the front and back of the popover. If using discarded plastic-bag handles, attach fringe strips *before* stapling the handles to the front and back of the popover.

7. To give a more finished look, tape the last strip of fringe to the popover with double-sided tape across the front and back top edges, so that it covers the staples holding the straps front and back.

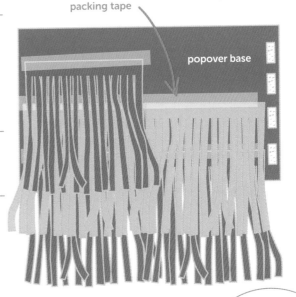

packing tape

popover base

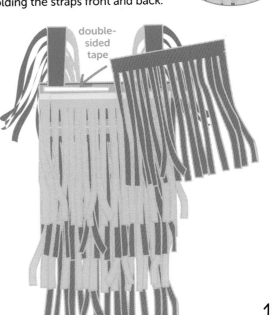

staple

double-sided tape

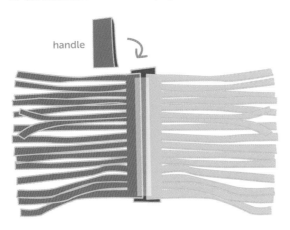

handle

11

CAPES

The superhero, witch, and gladiator costumes use style number one, while the vampire and magician costumes use style number two. Both are totally easy to make.

CAPE NUMBER ONE: BASIC RED SATIN

1. Cut cape material (red satin for superheroes or gladiator, black garbage bag for witch) to your desired width and length, adding an extra 3 inches to the length. Run a strip of double-sided tape across the top width of the material.

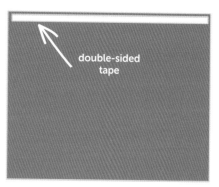

double-sided tape

2. Fold top over 2 inches, sticking tape to fabric to create a tunnel.

Fold over.

3. Tear or cut a 1-inch-wide strip of material from the bottom of the cape for a drawstring.

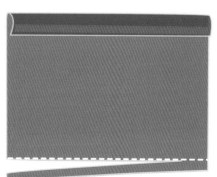

4. Attach a safety pin or a paper clip to one end of the drawstring. Use the pin or clip to feed the drawstring through the tunnel.

safety pin

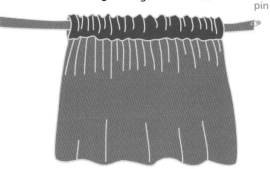

5. Adjust the gathers on the cape. Slip two pieces of double-sided tape just inside the openings of the tunnel and stick down so that the cape remains at a set width. Trim drawstring tails to 1 inch, attach two, 1-inch pieces of fastener strips to the ends, with the corresponding fastener strips attached to costume shoulders.

fastener

double-sided tape

fastener

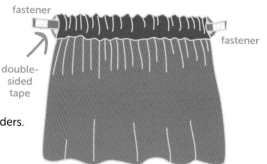

12

CAPE NUMBER TWO:
RED-SATIN-LINED, COLLARED CAPE

1. Cut off one side of a black plastic garbage bag to the desired width and length of your cape. Lay it flat on your work surface. Run a line of double-sided tape across the top width edge of the bag. To make the collar outline, run two 5-inch-long strips of double-sided tape down from each corner as shown. Finish the collar outline, with a second horizontal strip of double-sided tape as shown. Leave a 1-inch space and then outline the rest of the cape in double-sided tape.

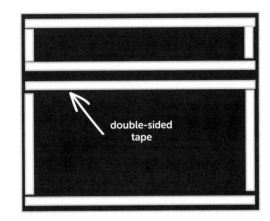

double-sided tape

2. Peel away the paper on the double-sided tape. Cut out a piece of satin slightly larger than the garbage bag.

red satin

3. With a partner, lower the satin onto the bag so that it sticks to the tape. Trim the edges right up to or even on the tape. The tape will keep the red satin from fraying.

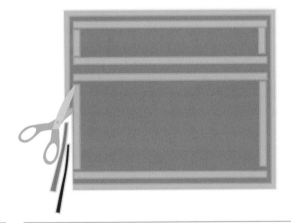

4. Pin a safety pin to the end of a ribbon. Use the pin to help feed the ribbon through the pocket.

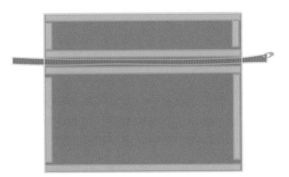

5. Draw the ribbon through the pocket, trim the ends, and tie.

13

WIGS AND WILD HAIR

In the book, you will find curling-ribbon wigs used with the princess, goddess, and Egyptian queen costumes, but really this wig-making technique can be used with any costume where you want more hair—anywhere! You can even make cool beards using this technique. On the facing page, the torn-T-shirt wigs produce a completely different look.

CURLING-RIBBON WIGS

1. Cut a strip of mesh drawer liner or a rug pad long enough to fit around your head. If it is going to attach to a band (goddess wig), make it ¾ inch wide. If it will be taped inside a hat (princess wig) make it 2 inches wide.

mesh drawer liner
or rug pad

2. Wrap the strip around your forehead, marking where you want to start the curls— your temples are a good place.

3. Cut pieces of curling ribbon two times as long as your desired length; none have to be exact. Fold the ribbon in half, thread the center through a hole in the mesh, and pull the ends through the loop, knotting it into the mesh. Fill up the strip as densely as you like.

4. For the goddess wreath/headband and the Egyptian queen, we loop shorter lengths of ribbon on the top row to spill over the top of the band and crown. For the princess hat, we use only the bottom rows. You can also use this curling technique on a hair elastic and add ribbon curls to your own curls!

curling ribbon, folded in half

Poke folded center through mesh.

Pull ends through loop and tighten to make knot.

ROPY DREADLOCKS (PIRATE, CLOWN, AND WITCH COSTUMES)

 Cut an old T-shirt straight across under the arms. Then cut both sides, so you are left with two rectangular pieces.

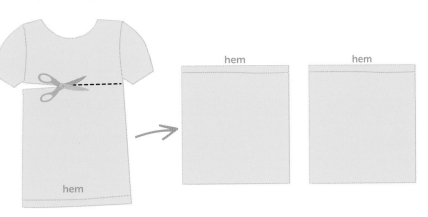

 All along the top cut edge of one of the T-shirt rectangles, make 1- to 2-inch vertical cuts about 1 to 2 inches apart. Tear the shirt from each cut all the way to the hem of the shirt. Fold this strip of T-shirt fringe in half and tape or glue it together so it's double thick. Repeat with the second T-shirt rectangle.

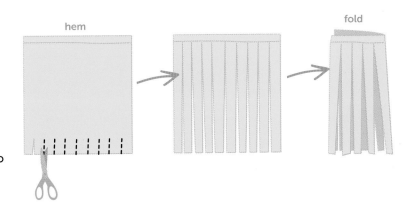

Tape or glue the T-shirt hair into the hat (witch and clown), or head scarf (pirate).

Trim hair to a length you like.

STRAIGHT HIPPIE HAIR

Use the dreadlock method, but instead of tearing the T-shirt fabric, cut the strands the whole way. The closer together the cuts, the thinner and more hairlike the wig will look.

15

FEATHERS, FLOWERS, AND LEAVES

These techniques are used for the flapper, princess, fairy, goddess, mermaid, hula girl, hippies, and even chicken costume.

FEATHER

1. Accordion-fold a rectangular piece of plastic bag. Staple in a line down the center of the folded piece.

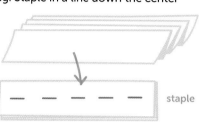

staple

2. Fold in half along the strip of staples. Draw a long oval shape curving around the staples as. Cut out.

3. Make a lot of feathery cuts as shown, being careful to stop before the staple line.

4. Cut out a skinny piece of cardboard in the shape shown. Glue it over the staples. Fluff the "feathers."

FLOWER

1. Cut a strip of plastic bag to approximately 3 inches by 15 inches. Accordian-fold the strip. Stick a straight pin through the center and draw a petal shape around the pin. Cut out the shape.

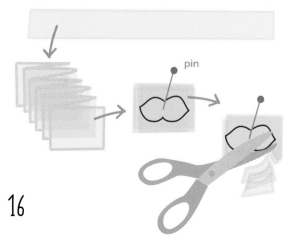

pin

2. With the pin in place, spin the petals out in a shape you like. Remove the pin, and staple the center, or staple directly to a ribbon headband. (If that is what you are making, see page 43.) Cut a small circle from a different color plastic bag. Glue over the staple.

LEAVES AND LAUREL CROWN

1. THE HEADBAND: Cut a 2½-by-15-inch strip of green plastic bag long enough to fit around your head with a bit of overlap. To close the crown, attach a fastener strip to each end. Open the headband and lay it flat on your work surface. You can also make wrist and ankle ruffles by following these steps. Just use a smaller piece of green plastic, punch holes at the ends and fasten with green ribbon or green plastic ties.

fastener   fastener

2. THE LEAVES: Cut a strip of green plastic bag to approximately 2½ by 2½ inches, then accordian-fold it. Stick a straight pin through the center and draw a leaf shape around the pin. Cut out the shape. Repeat with several different shades of green plastic bag.

Repeat with different colors.

3. ATTACHING LEAVES: Run a strip of double-sided tape down the center of the headband. Starting at one end of the headband, stick the leaves to the tape, overlapping shapes and mixing up the greens, so that only the bottoms of the leaf shapes are stuck to the tape.

double-sided tape

ATTACHING CURLS

1. Run a strip of double-sided tape down the inside center of the headband. Attach the mesh strip (see page 14) to the headband. Arrange the short strands so they flow over the top of the headband in a pleasing way.

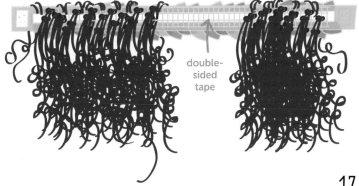

double-sided tape

17

PLUCKY PRINCESS

move over, Rapunzel! Anyone can be a princess with long, flowing locks and a sweeping skirt! The ball-gown skirt is made from an inexpensive plastic tablecloth. We chose blue, because our princess had a light blue leotard for the top; but plastic cloths come in a wide variety of colors. Don't have a leotard? A formfitting, long-sleeved T-shirt will work. To make the skirt, follow the directions on page 6. To make the hat and decorative flowers for the top, follow the directions on page 16. To make the wrist ruffles, follow the instructions on page 6 and make two teeny skirts. The ones in the photograph use the elastic threading technique on page 5.

1. Cut a sheet of poster board to 12 inches by 22 inches.

2. Roll the sheet into a cone shape, connecting the two bottom corners.

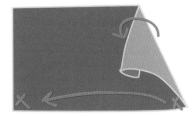

3. Inside of the hat, tape the bottom corners together plus a few more spots up the inseam to keep the roll in place.

tape →

4. Using a straight edge, draw a line from the top of the hat to the overlapping corners at the bottom. Run a strip of double-sided tape down that line and seal the outer seam. Trim away the extra flap.

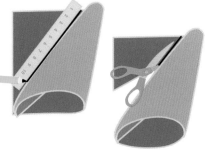

5. Cut a piece of plastic bag as shown.

6. Scrunch up the top edge of the bag and stick it into the small hole at the top of the cone. Tape on the inside to hold.

7. Use double-sided tape to attach a strip of ribbon around the base of the hat.

8. Following the directions on page 16, make one plastic flower. Using double-sided tape, attach it to the hat wherever you like. Make a few more flowers. Attach them to the top of the leotard or T-shirt with paper clips taped to the backs of the flowers.

9. To make the long, luxurious curls (of any color), follow the directions on page 14. Attach them to the inside of the hat with double-sided tape.

10. Fasten the hat to your head with two bobby pins.

VALIANT KNIGHT

It's easy to suit up for dragon slaying. First stop is the linen closet for a solid-color pillowcase. The knight's underpinnings are just a simple solid-color, long sleeved T-shirt and leggings. Read on for instructions to make a pattern for a basic symbol to put on a knight's tunic and shield. Knights identified themselves by their coats of arms, which are interesting to learn about. If you had a coat of arms, what would it look like?

TUNIC

1. Cut openings for the knight's arms and head along the pillowcase seams, as shown. The armholes measure 6½ inches long by about 2 inches wide.

Trim armholes in blue duct tape. Tuck the fabric around the neck opening back into the costume and secure it with double-sided tape.

6½ inches

1½–2 inches

pillowcase

1½–2 inches

6½ inches

2. To make the knightly hem pattern at the bottom: Flatten the pillowcase on your work surface. First, cut and tape side slits using the same dimensions as the armholes.

3. Using three-inch strips of blue duct tape, create the pattern shown below. Cut the center sections as shown.

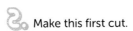

3 inches

3 inches

3 inches

HERALDIC PATTERN

1. Fold a 7-by-7-inch piece of paper in half and then in half again, as shown.

2. Make this first cut.

3. Make these two cuts; unfold pattern.

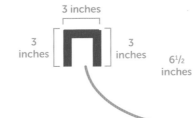

heraldic pattern

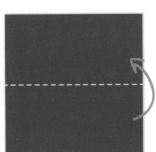

4. Trace this shape on a contrasting-color material. Cut it out and glue to the tunic.

21

KNIGHTLY EQUIPMENT

SHOULDER SHIELDS

1. Begin by collecting two foam vegetable containers (mushroom boxes are a good source) plus two cartons lined with silvery cardboard (such as boxed soups or drinks or cardboard cracker containers rinsed clean).

2. Cut off one side of a foam container, as shown. Place it bottom-up on your work surface.

3. Cut out three strips of silvery cardboard into the shapes shown below. Wrap and staple the rectangular strip around the sides of the container.

4. Overlap and staple the two triangular pieces to cover the container's bottom, as shown.

open side

5. Using double-sided tape, overlap foil yogurt or pudding tops along the bottom edge of the shoulder pad as shown. Attach shields to shoulders, with 1 inch of fastener strips.

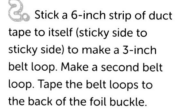

yogurt tops

BELT BUCKLE

1. Using double-sided tape, overlap and tape together four square foil yogurt or pudding tops turned on an angle, as shown. Run a strip of duct tape across the back of all four tops.

2. Stick a 6-inch strip of duct tape to itself (sticky side to sticky side) to make a 3-inch belt loop. Make a second belt loop. Tape the belt loops to the back of the foil buckle.

3. Run a plain belt through the belt loops. Buckle the belt in the back; position the foil buckle front and center.

SHIELD

1. Use a clean shallow aluminum pan for the shield. The outside bottom of the pan is the front of the shield. Decorate with black dot stickers, plastic coins, and a paper tracing of the heraldic symbol. Attach with double-sided tape or craft glue.

2. Make shield handles out of duct tape strips or craft foam strips attached to the inside of the pan.

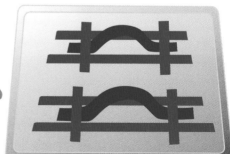

STALWART SWORD

The sword is used by this valiant knight as well as by the gutsy gladiator (page 30) and the swashbuckling pirate (page 34). Easy to make, it looks almost real, with its aged handle and shiny blade!

1. Cut a piece of cardboard into the shape below.

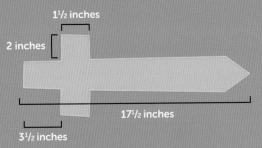

1½ inches

2 inches

17½ inches

3½ inches

2. Glue a paint-stirring stick where the handle meets the blade. This will keep the sword from bending.

3. Run double-sided tape down the edges of both sides of the blade and wrap the entire blade in aluminum foil.

4. Wrap the handle with strips of masking tape. Rub a dark-color shoe polish into the tape to stain it, then wipe off the extra with an old rag.

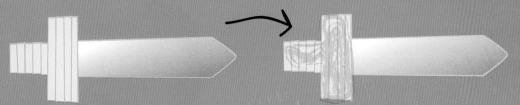

23

QUEEN OF HEARTS

Target bags plus an extra-large trash bag equals a costume fit for a queen! If you don't have Target bags, you can use white trash bags and decorate with red heart stickers. A black leotard is the base. A formfitting, long-sleeved black T-shirt will also work. Decorate with hearts cut from sticky-back felt or glittery stickers.

NECK RUFF

1. To make the neck ruff, use the skirt instructions on page 5 to connect eight medium Target bags. Cut 9 inches off the bottom of the connected bag strip. (Cut along the dot pattern to create a scalloped edge.)

2. Instead of elastic cord, thread a 40-inch red shoelace through the holes. Bunch the bags up in the middle to create the ruffle. Place the ruffle behind your neck, with the scalloped edge pointing up. Run the shoelace under your arms and tie in the back.

back

1. Flatten an extra-large trash or contractor bag. Tape the bag to your work surface as shown. Cut a rounded corner that runs from the upper-right top to the lower-left bottom.

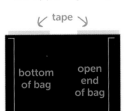

2. Open the newly cut shape on your work surface. Create a hole-punch waistband using the method on page 5 across the flat edge.

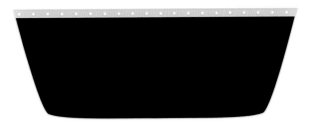

3. Connect three large Target bags using the bag skirt instructions on page 5. Cut along the dot pattern to create a scalloped edge at the hem.

4. Lay the connected Target bags on top of the black bag, as shown. Fold the sides of the black bag in, overlapping the Target bags. Run a ribbon through the holes (starting at the center back and then working around to the front, one side at a time) and through both the Target and black bag layers at the front of the skirt.

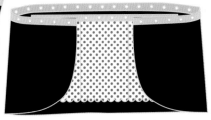

CROWN

Cut a 4-by-24-inch-long band of silver poster board. Cut a scallop pattern down one long side of the band. Measure the spot where the band overlaps (by about an inch) wrapped around your head. Mark it with a pencil. Cut off the extra. Use fastener strips to close the ends of the crown. To make the silver stripe, run a strip of double-sided tape down the center of the band and sprinkle the sticky strip with lots of silver glitter. Cut a big red heart from shiny red paper or glitter one yourself. Glue it to the front of the crown.

HEART STAFF

Use packing tape to attach three or four cardboard wrapping-paper tubes together. Run strips of double-sided tape up and down the rolls. Cover the connected rolls in aluminum foil. Wrap black duct tape or electrical tape in a spiral down the length of the aluminum foil staff. Top off with a heart-shape Valentine's candy box (or two glittered-hearts) glued or taped to the top of the staff.

inside box

glue

top lid attached

CARD SOLDIER

For the card player in the family, this costume is a no-brainer. Base pieces are a red hoodie and red sweat pants pushed up to resemble breeches over a pair of striped tights or kneesocks. Red leggings would work, too.

1. The costume itself is just a decorated sandwich board—we used foam core, but poster board will work. Size can vary. This one is 15 inches wide by 24 inches long. Decorate front and back to look like your favorite playing card. We cut the shiny hearts from an old gift bag. You can also use wrapping paper or construction paper.

2. For shoulder straps, cut two pieces of ribbon, 12 to 20 inches long. Use double-sided tape to attach the ribbons to the inside of the front and back of the cards with at least 3 inches of ribbon glued inside. (Measure the length of the ribbons so that the sandwich board hangs around knee level.)

packing tape on top of ribbons

double-sided tape underneath ribbons

3. For extra support, run a piece of packing tape across the ribbon at the very top edge of the card. Attach a 17-to-24-inch piece of ribbon to the middle of the interior sides of the front and back boards and tie them as shown.

BEE-UTIFUL BEE

You need a yellow leotard (or snug yellow T-shirt) and black tights to bee-gin transforming into a bee.

SKIRT

Begin with a yellow plastic tablecloth or inexpensive shower curtain. Follow the tunnel waistband skirt instructions on page 7, step 1. Then, turn the material over to its front and run black electrical tape across its width to make stripes. Return to steps 2 through 4 to finish the skirt.

ANTENNAE

To make antennae bulbs, take 2½-inch-long strips of leftover yellow plastic and roll them up. Tape at the ends to make two bulbs. Attach each yellow bulb to the ends of two lengths of craft wire with black electrical tape.

RUFFLE CUFFS

To make a wrist ruffle cuff, accordion-fold 3 inches by 12 inches of the same yellow material you used for the skirt. Cut a wavy shape across the bottom, which will create a petal effect when the accordion is opened. Follow the ribbon skirt instructions on page 6. Repeat for the second cuff.

WINGS

1. Bend medium-weight craft wire into two pairs of wing shape. Leave about 3 inches of extra wire at the end of each wing pair.

2. Cut the legs off two pairs of black tights (we use fishnets and patterned ones). Stretch one leg over each wire shape. Tie each leg in a knot at the bottom to keep it in place.

3. Twist the wires together around a central point. Arrange the wings as shown. Wrap the middle with another piece of tights or a length of ribbon to cover the wire-wrapped center.

4. Tie two 47-inch shoelaces, or ribbons, to the center. To secure, loop one shoelace over right shoulder, under arm, and tie in back on right side. Do the same on the left side.

two shoelaces (or ribbon)

27

FANCIFUL FAIRY

Flit your way around the house in this ethereal fairy costume. A flesh-colored leotard is the best base. To make the skirt and top, use thin small-can liners, which come in a wide range of colors, often on a roll, and yellow grocery bags. To make the wings, use the same plastic liners for the wing covers, and follow the instructions on page 27.

SKIRT

1. Cut liner to the desired length, trimming extra from the open end. Fold in half the long way and cut a leaf-point shape at the open end.

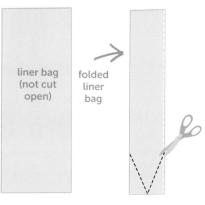

liner bag (not cut open)   folded liner bag

2. Unfold the liner you just trimmed and shaped. Add a shorter layer in front using the same method. (We used a yellow grocery bag cut to the same width as the unfolded green bags.) Attach the top edge of the short bag to the top edge of the longer bag with double-sided tape.

double-sided tape   smaller layer

3. Fold both bags over 1½ inches and tape with masking tape. Slide elastic cord (see measuring tip, page 4) through the tunnel.

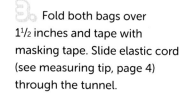

4. Keep making and adding petal sections to the elastic until the skirt fits around your waist and is pleasingly full. Tie elastic in a knot.

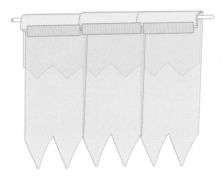

TOP

Use the same method for making skirt petals to make the top petals. Top strips will simply be a bit shorter, and you will need fewer sets. Rather than running the petal sections onto an elastic, string them onto a ribbon. You may decide to use double-sided tape or clear tape to tape the seams together once you put your costume on.

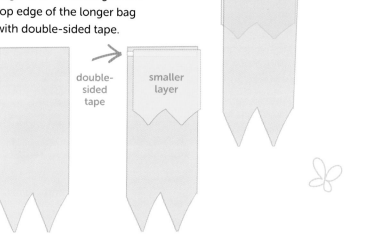

ribbon instead of elastic

shorter layers, taped in back

1. Accordion-fold a thin plastic liner bag. Cut a leaf shape at the open end of the bag. Repeat with the second color bag, cutting out a smaller leaf shape.

folded-up liner bags

FLOWERS:
To make the flowers, follow the instructions on page 16. Use double-sided tape or glue to stick each one to the top of a hair clip or barrette.

2. Open the accordion. Layer the leaf strips, one on top of the other, and attach with double-sided tape.

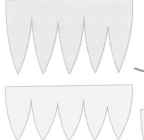

double-sided tape

3. Repeat for the second ankle ruffle.

4. Follow the hole punch skirt instructions on page 5, steps 3 and 4, to finish the two ankle ruffles.

masking tape on back, punch holes every inch, run string through, gather, and tie

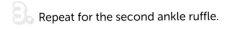

29

GUTSY GLADIATOR

C ollect these costume materials and you are ready to become a roman gladiator: brown paper bags (or craft paper sheets), a heavy plastic trash bag, shiny gold Mylar snack bags, and an extra-long shoelace or ribbon. A long-sleeve black T-shirt and leggings are all that are needed to wear underneath the costume.

GLADIATOR CAPE

Make the basic cape design on page 12 using the red satin that comes with this kit. Attach it to your shoulders with fastener strips.

SWORD AND SHIELD

Make the sword on page 23. Make a shield similar to the one on page 22 (for the knight). Since gladiators' shields were generally round, use a divided round aluminum supermarket tray for the basic shield. To decorate, glue on coins or bottle caps. The handles are the same as the ones for the knight's shield.

STUDDED COLLAR

1. Trace the outline of a 14-inch round (bowl, pot lid, bucket) on brown craft paper. Cut out the circle. Trace a smaller circle in the middle—the small circle should be big enough to fit around your neck. Cut a slit from the outer to the inner circle. Cut out the inner circle completely.

2. Punch holes all around the collar. The big holes on our collar are made with a ½-inch hole punch, then backed with squares of gold Mylar (cut from shiny Mylar snack bags) and taped to the back of the collar so the gold shows through the hole. The small holes are made with a small hole punch.

3. Tape the collar to a piece of heavy black plastic using double-sided tape. Cut around the edges of both the outside and the inside neck rings, leaving a tiny bit of the black plastic showing as trim. The black plastic bag showing through the small holes will look like studs.

14-inch circle

gold Mylar taped to back

front

black plastic bag

front

WAR SKIRT

1. Cut strips of bag or craft paper 2½ inches wide and 17 inches long. Trim the ends to a point.

17 inches

2.5 inches

2. Decorate the strips any way you like. We continued using the ½-inch hole-punch design backed with gold Mylar. Fold over the top 2 inches of each strip to its wrong side and secure with tape.

tape

front

back

gold Mylar

3. Feed the strips onto a shoelace long enough to tie around your waist. Make as many decorated strips as you need to fit all the way around your waist. Tie the war skirt in the back.

WRIST CUFFS

Cut open two brown cardboard coffee-cup sleeves. Snip off a bit of each sleeve so it almost fits around your wrist. Punch holes across the top and down two sides as shown. Starting in the center hole on the top edge, weave a single long shoelace across the top (to the right and to the left). When you get to the side holes criss-cross the laces across the opening in the cuff, as if you were lacing shoes. Slip your hand in and tie.

GLORIOUS GODDESS AND EGYPTIAN QUEEN

Watch out, Helen of Troy and Cleopatra! Cut up three white short-sleeve adult T-shirts as shown and turn yourself into the most perfect goddess or the bravest Egyptian queen on either side of the Mediterranean Sea!

GODDESS CURLS AND LAUREL CROWN

To create the long goddess curls with laurel leaf crown, follow the instructions on page 14 for the curls and page 17 for the crown.

GODDESS CORDED BELT

Depending on your size, cut a 2- to 3-yard length of silk cord or pretty ribbon. Bring the cord around your waist, from the back to the front, and tie the first knot. Send each end over its respective shoulder. Tie the ends in the back to the waistband to finish the look.

DRESS

1. For the very first layer, wear a white sleeveless T-shirt that's just your size. Put the big T-shirts on in the order of their numbers. Cut up each T-shirt as shown.

2. **T-shirt #1** Wear T-shirt #1 with the neck hole around your waist as a skirt.

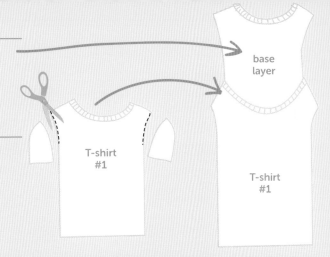

base layer

T-shirt #1

T-shirt #1

3. **T-shirt #2** Cut away the neck band. Cut a V-neck in the front and back of the T-shirt. Wear T-shirt #2 over your fitted shirt.

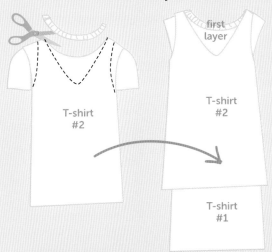

first layer

T-shirt #2

T-shirt #2

T-shirt #1

4. **T-shirt #3** Cut off the sleeves from under the arm to about 2 to 3 inches from the neck opening. Wear T-shirt #3 over T-shirt #2.

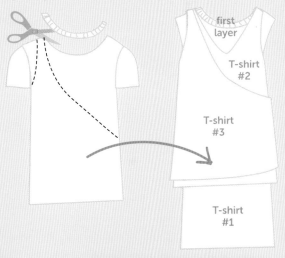

first layer

T-shirt #2

T-shirt #3

T-shirt #1

EGYPTIAN QUEEN COLLAR AND WRIST CUFF

Follow the instructions on page 31 to make the collar. In addition to the gold Mylar circles, glue on jewels in a pattern you like. Follow the instructions on page 31 to make one wrist cuff. Measure it to fit around your wrist with a bit of overlap rather than snipping it short. Close the cuff with fastener strips. Decorate with glue-on jewels.

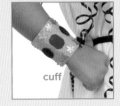

cuff

EGYPTIAN QUEEN CROWN

There are several styles of crown fit for an Egyptian queen. Here we use a single strip of gold cardboard with a center section that juts up above the forehead. Cut to fit around the head and close with fastener strips in the back. Decorate with glue-on jewels and shiny paper. Make a curling-ribbon wig and attach it to the inside of the crown (see page 17).

SWASHBUCKLING PIRATES

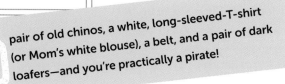
pair of old chinos, a white, long-sleeved-T-shirt (or Mom's white blouse), a belt, and a pair of dark loafers—and you're practically a pirate!

Cut off the chinos below the knee with a jagged edge. Make the simple vest on page 8. Rip up the dreadlock T-shirt wig on page 15 and attach it to a pirate-worthy scarf to tie around your head. Add a string of beads along with an old hoop earring to one side of the scarf-wig. Cut a strip of red satin from the piece that comes with this kit and tie it around your waist. Make the sword on page 23. Follow the directions below to make the bandolier and shoe buckles. Look fierce.

BANDOLIER AND SHOE BUCKLES

1. You will need brown and bronze paper to make the buckles.

> buckle base: brown paper rectangle with rounded edges

2. Cut the base of whichever item you are making to the desired size. The bandolier buckle base should be 3½ inches by 5 inches. The shoe buckle bases should each be 2½ inches by 3 inches. Round off the corners. Fold a piece of white paper the same size as the base piece, but fold it into quarters.

white paper

Fold into quarters.

Draw a wavy line from one folded edge to the other folded edge.

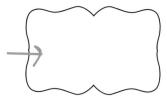

3. Trace the decorative buckle shape onto the bronze paper. Cut it out and glue to the brown paper.

Glue bronze paper shape onto brown paper.

4. Make two slits. For shoes, feed a strip of black paper or craft foam through the slits and tape a paper clip to the back. Clip to shoes.

paper clip

tape

back of buckle

5. For bandolier, feed onto belt. Strap belt over one shoulder and buckle in the back.

striped tights, a red leotard (or long-sleeved shirt), and a pair of boots, and you are on your way to becoming a bold buccaneer! Follow the skirt instructions on page 5. Make the bag vest on page 8, closing it up with bright red laces. Cut a strip wide enough to tie around your head, pirate-style, from the piece of red satin that comes with this kit. Make the sword on page 23. Look dangerous.

MERMAID

A flesh-colored leotard makes the best base for this wavy lady. To make her leafy crown, follow the instructions on page 17. To make the beautiful seashell top, which is also in fashion with hula girls, turn to page 38.

MERMAID TAIL

1. You will need to take two measurements to make your mermaid skirt pattern. Measure the distance from your waist to the floor and add 1 inch. This is your pattern length. Measure your waist and add 16 inches. This is your pattern width. Cut a piece of newspaper, craft paper, or wrapping paper that is that width by that height and fold it in half.

2. Measure and mark the specific points (see drawing). Then connect the dots to create a fat fishy shape along the fold. Cut it out, lay flat, and voilà—you have your tail pattern.

width = your waist measurement + 16 inches

craft paper or newspaper

length = distance from waist to floor + 1 inch

1½ inches

5 inches

fold

2 inches

5 inches

4 inches

2 inches

mermaid tail pattern

3. Trace the pattern onto an inexpensive shower-curtain liner and cut out the fish.

green shower-curtain liner

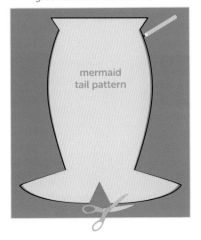

mermaid tail pattern

4. Line the edges of the tail with double-sided tape. Lay the skirt on another rectangular piece of the shower curtain liner. Fold back half the tail, peel off the tape, and stick it down. Do the same to the other side. Use edging scissors (optional) to trim away the extra material all around mermaid skirt. Take a minute to slip into your fishy tail and make sure it fits.

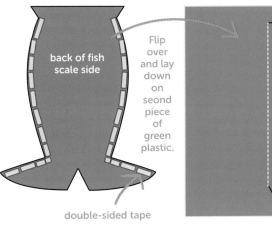

back of fish scale side

Flip over and lay down on seond piece of green plastic.

double-sided tape

5. If you would like, add scales and decorate your fins. Create a template by cutting a scalloped pattern on a strip of poster board. Lay the skirt flat and draw scales on your fish using the template and a dark green marker. Draw stripes on the fins.

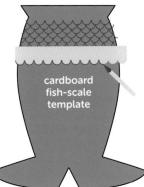

cardboard fish-scale template

6. Run a piece of clear packing tape inside and up the center back of the skirt. Cut a slit up the center of the tape. (This is to help you walk in the skinny mermaid skirt.)

clear packing tape

7. To make the waistband, follow the instructions on page 6.

See the next page for the seashell top.

HULA GIRL

Our hula lovely decided she also needed long, luxurious curls. To get the same effect, follow the instructions on page 14 and 17. You can make leafy wrist and ankle cuffs to complete the look by using the instuctions on page 17.

SEASHELL TOP

1. Cut slits in the tops of two round, cardboard cheese-box lids.

2. Make six slits as shown. Run a length of ribbon, long enough to tie around your rib cage, through the four A slits. Secure with duct tape. Run a length of ribbon through each B slit, long enough to tie behind your neck, and secure with duct tape.

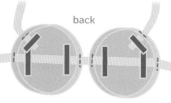

front

back

3. Cut shell shapes out of craft foam. Stick shell shapes to the tops with double-sided tape.

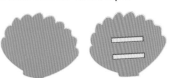

HULA SKIRT

1. Cut a wheat-colored jersey pillowcase up to the hem using the same technique as we use to make hippie hair on page 15.

2. To make the waistband, cut two small slits in the hem of the pillowcase, about an inch apart. Feed a ribbon (with a safety pin on one end) in through one slit, around the hem, and out through the other slit.

small slits in hem

ribbon with safety pin

Cut open sewn end of pillowcase.

Cut skinny strips up to hem across whole pillowcase.

38

WILY WITCH AND VICIOUS VAMPIRE

WILY WITCH

Double, double toil and trouble...a pinch of pirate...a whiff of wolf...and pouf—a witch! The vest is the same as the pirate girl's on page 35. The skirt is the same as the wolf girl's on page 58. To make the cape, follow the directions on page 12. To grow long green hair, follow the directions on page 15, then glue the locks inside the headband of a store-bought witch's hat. Add stripy leggings and a long-sleeved red T-shirt and you are ready to hop on a broomstick.

VICIOUS VAMPIRE

Even the vilest vampire can be counted on to be a snazzy dresser. A crisp white shirt, black pants, and black shoes from your own closet are the base. Make the cape on page 13.

CUMMERBUND

1. Cut a strip of red satin that comes with the kit (or red plastic tablecloth) 15 inches wide and long enough to wrap around your waist with 3 to 4 extra inches.

2. Flatten the material on your work surface. Pull up a fold every few inches along the length as shown. Secure with masking tape every few inches. Fold over any raw edges and tape down with masking tape.

masking tape

back of cummerbund

Store-bought glow-in-the-dark teeth are optional.

3. On the front side, slip a few pieces of double-sided tape between the folds. Wrap around your waist and secure with fastener strips.

fastener

double-sided tape

front of cummerbund

fastener

NINJA, TWO WAYS

NINJA #1

1. The base pieces are a black hooded sweatshirt, leggings or sweats, black socks, and black sneakers.

2. Cut an XL adult-size black T-shirt into a tunic, as shown.

3. Pop the tunic over your black top and bottom. Tie on the ninja belt (see page 41) or a red sash cut from the fabric that comes with the kit.

Ninja #1

It doesn't take much to get into ninja fighting form.

GLOVES

Cut a pair of black knee-high socks as shown.

Do not cut here.

Ninja #2

NINJA #2

1. The base pieces are an adult-size long-sleeved black T-shirt, black leggings or sweatpants, and black boots.

2. Cut off the sleeves and across the lower half of a too-small hooded black sweatshirt as shown. (If there is a logo on it, turn it inside out.)

3. Pop the hoodie over black top and bottom. Tie on the ninja belt (see page 41) or a red sash cut from the fabric that comes with the kit.

NINJA ACCESSORIES

BELT WITH STARS

1. Cut a 2-inch-wide strip of plastic garbage bag long enough to wrap around your body and tie.

2. Fold clean yogurt-top circles into quarters or eighths. Cut star shapes, as shown. Layer the stars to make them more interesting. Attach them to the belt with a brad fastener.

yogurt-top circle

brad fastener

2-inch-wide strip of plastic garbage bag

SWORD

1. Run double-sided tape down one side of an extra-large paint-stirring stick. Wrap the stick in aluminum foil.

foil

2. Place two pieces of double-sided tape on the handle. Cut a 2-inch-wide strip from a black plastic bag and wrap it around the handle only. Attach with double-sided tape.

SHEATH

1. Staple one end of a paper-towel roll closed. Paint it black. Wrap a band of duct tape about a ½ inch down from the open end.

duct tape

2. Cut two slits in the duct tape section on the sheath. Run an end of the star belt through the slits.

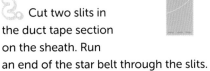

duct tape with two slits

belt

sheath

NUNCHUCKS (AKA NUNCHAKU)

paper clip

1. Cut a paper-towel roll open. Lay flat. Reinforce the upper-left corner with tape. Punch a hole and slip a paper clip through the hole. Run a strip of double-sided tape along the right edge.

2. Starting from the left side (the side with the paper clip), roll up the cardboard very tightly. Use the tape to stick closed.

3. Place a square piece of masking tape over each open end of the roll.

tape

4. Cut little slits all around the tape square as shown, and fold down around the open ends.

5. Make a second one. Paint both black. Connect with a paper-clip chain.

VERY COOL HIPPIES

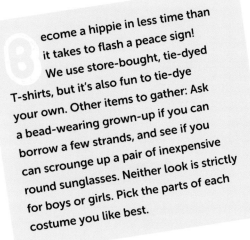

Become a hippie in less time than it takes to flash a peace sign! We use store-bought, tie-dyed T-shirts, but it's also fun to tie-dye your own. Other items to gather: Ask a bead-wearing grown-up if you can borrow a few strands, and see if you can scrounge up a pair of inexpensive round sunglasses. Neither look is strictly for boys or girls. Pick the parts of each costume you like best.

HIPPIE BOY

Make the fringed vest on page 9. Make the long, straight hippie hair on page 15. Attach the hair with double-sided tape to a headband (or strip of fabric) that ties around your head. Wear jeans.

HIPPIE GIRL

Make the fringed vest on page 9. NOTE: The bottom fringe is cut much longer than it is on the other vest. To make a cool closing: Punch two holes on either side of the vest. Lace a ribbon or shoelace through the holes. String a few plastic beads onto the ends of the ribbon. Knot the ribbon ends to hold beads. Make the flowers on page 16 and staple them to a ribbon that ties around your head. Duct tape the backs of the staples inside the ribbon so the staples don't scratch your head.

1. Cut triangle pieces from the bottoms of a pair of old jeans.

2. Use the cutout denim pieces as guidelines to cut triangles from a different fabric—we use old skirt fabric. The new triangles should be wider than the denim guides.

Trace each triangle, add a little extra on all sides, and cut out. If possible, match new triangles with the cutout spots for best fit.

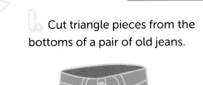

3. Turn the jeans inside out. (Place a piece of waxed paper or scrap paper inside the pant leg to protect the other side from glue drips.) Line the cut edges of the jeans with fabric glue. Glue new fabric triangles to openings—wrong side of fabric should be up.

inside-out jean legs

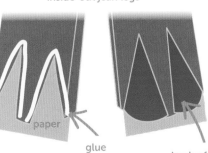

paper

glue

back of new triangle

4. Let dry and turn right side out; decorate with fabric markers.

43

SPECTACULAR SPACE PEOPLE

Before you pretend to check out the nearest galaxy, suit up in a space costume and far-out space accessories you make yourself.

SPACE VEST

1. Use a large-size bubble mailer bag to make the space vest. Cut a semicircle shape into the middle of the closed end of the envelope, leaving about one inch of envelope from each edge.

2. Cut open the sides of the envelope.

3. Cut two side strips from the piece you cut out (or from a new envelope altogether). Line up the short edge of a strap with a side edge of the vest, midway down one side of the vest. Staple together. Pop the vest over your head. Attach fastener squares to the side strip and the vest. Repeat for other side strap. Decorate with blue duct tape from this kit.

SPACE CUFFS

Cut out two pieces of Bubble Wrap or envelope mailer about 5 to 7 inches wide and as long as it needs to be to wrap around your wrist or forearm and overlap by at least 1½ inches. Decorate with tape. Close with fasteners.

1. Cut a long cardboard tube (we used a wrapping-paper tube) in half. Wrap aluminum foil around each half to make the booster rockets.

2. Using a paper-towel tube as a spacer, tape the three tubes together. Wrap a piece of Bubble Wrap around the three tubes to cover the center tube.

3. Glue on plastic juice-container tops and colored plastic cups to the bottom of each rocket, and plastic domes from the quarter machines you find at supermarkets to the top.

4. Decorate the body with colored caps for dials, and precut foam numbers.

5. Run ribbons for straps through the center paper towel holder and tie at a comfortable length—like a backpack.

SPACE SKIRT

To make the Bubble Wrap skirt, follow the ribbon sash skirt instructions on page 6.

HELMET

Peal the plastic shell off an old bike helmet. Decorate with markers, tape, and knobs. Use craft wire run through the helmet holes and around a cork to make the antenna and mic. Wrap aluminum foil around the wire frame to fill out the antennae and wrap more around the cork mic. To make the chin strap, weave a strip of Bubble Wrap or mailer bag through the helmet and secure inside with tape. connect under chin with fastener strips.

SPACE RADIO

Use an egg carton for the base. Wrap it in aluminum foil using double-sided tape to secure it. Decorate with tape, stickers, lids, caps, and mesh from a vegetable bag. Attach a foil-covered chopstick to the side of the radio with double-sided tape.

RAY BLASTER

Attach three colored plastic cups with double-sided tape. Decorate with blue duct tape and bottle caps. Tape an empty tape dispenser to the cups for a handle.

45

...ASTIC FLAPPER

...lappers were high-spirited, ...ndependent young women in ...he 1920s whose style was as ...onary for their time as their ...w: no corsets, short skirts, ...ads, feathers, and fringe!

To become a modern-day flapper, follow the instructions for the fringed popover on page 10. This one is all white, but you can use any color or combination of colors you like. The shoulder straps and headband were cut from a bubble mailer bag. To make the feather, follow the instructions on page 16.

EYEBALL ALIEN

Aliens from another planet more your speed? Follow the same fringed popover instructions on page 10 using bags in a color combination that makes you smile.

EYEBALL HAT

1. Use a bag in one of the colors from the costume. Collect as many plastic domes as you can from those quarter machines you find at supermarkets.

bag (cut-off handles)

plastic domes

black paper circles

2. Cut out a bunch of different-size black circles, and drop one inside each dome. Stuff the dome with cotton or white tissue. Place the eyeball where you want it on the bag. Snap the top back on the dome from inside the bag, so that the plastic bag is in between the lid and the dome. Cover the hat in eyeballs large and small.

Snap on dome cap from inside bag.

3. Stuff the hat: Stuff another bag with tissue paper or packing peanuts, anything light and fluffy. Knot the bag and put it inside the alien hat.

4. Make and size the hatband: Cut a strip of poster board to fit around your head, and make it about 1½ to 2 inches wide. Size it to fit securely around your head and attach fastener strips to the ends to hold it in place. Starting at the front center of the hatband and the front center of the hat, and working outward in both directions, use double-sided tape to secure the headband to the inside of the alien hat. Gather and tape any extra bag in the back. Try the hat on. If it flops over, put more stuffing in the stuffing bag.

double-sided tape

Fold bottom of bag around headband.

To make the dress, follow the directions on page 10.

47

ROCK ON!

Be ready to strut your rock 'n' roll self once you create these supercool costumes. Strike a pose! Attitude is everything!

CUFF

Cut a piece of craft foam or black construction paper 2½ inches wide and as long as it needs to be to wrap around your wrist and overlap by 1½ inches. Punch holes along the edges of the cuff. Using double-sided tape, back the foam (or construction paper) with the Mylar interior of a snack bag cut to the same size as the cuff, so that the silver shows through the holes. Use fastener strips to close the cuff.

FLYING V GUITAR

1. To make a pattern for the body of the guitar, fold a piece of newsprint in half and put a tennis racket on top of it as shown.

ROCKER GIRL

The basic pieces you will need to become a rocker chick are short bike shorts or cutoff leggings plus a leotard or tight sleeveless T-shirt. Make the bag vest on page 8. Use extra-large safety pins to close the vest front. To make the skirt, follow the directions on page 5.

2. Trace a triangle around the racket that extends 2 inches below the bottom of the racket's face. Draw a diagonal line that extends from the lower-right corner of the triangle you just sketched to the bottom of the racket, as shown.

3. Cut out the triangle. When you get to the bottom, cut along the diagonal line. Unfold and lay flat.

5. For the top of the neck: Fold a 7-by-5-inch sheet of paper in half. Make a mark 2¼ inches from the fold. Then draw a rounded triangle shape along the fold.

fold

4. Using newsprint, cut out a pattern for the neck of the guitar, 2½ inches wide and as long as it needs to be to cover the handle of the tennis racket.

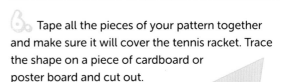

6. Tape all the pieces of your pattern together and make sure it will cover the tennis racket. Trace the shape on a piece of cardboard or poster board and cut out.

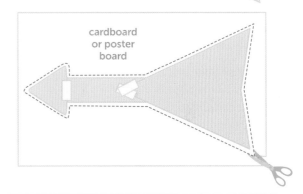

cardboard or poster board

DECORATE THE GUITAR

- The V-shaped base of the guitar is covered with a piece of shimmery paper from a larger gift bag. Then cut the V-pattern down smaller and glue on a second layer. (This one is white.)
- Cover the neck with black construction paper and the side edges of the top of the neck with black marker.
- Use a silver paint pen to draw six strings, as well as fret lines across the neck every 2 inches.
- The tuning pegs are glued-on paper clips.
- The knobs are glued-on bottle caps and paper.
- The studs are dots punched out of scraps of black construction paper.

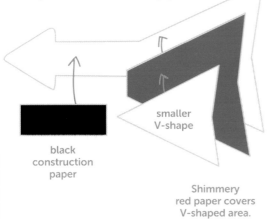

black construction paper

smaller V-shape

Shimmery red paper covers V-shaped area.

7. Trace the racket's shape on the back of the guitar. Tape pieces of craft wire onto the lines around the shape. Use the wires to attach the guitar to the racket.

ROCKER DUDE

Use what you have with attitude to become a rocker dude, then add the all-important accessories below to complete the look.

SAFETY-PIN PATCH

Cut a cool patch from a too-small T-shirt. Attach it with safety pins to a grown-up-size jean jacket, your own jeans, a plain T-shirt, or even our simple vest (see page 8).

HEADSET MIC

1. Cut a piece of craft wire about 15 inches long. Poke one end through a large black pom-pom. Fold the wire over the pom-pom, twist, and wrap with black electrical tape.

black electrical tape

craft wire

pom-pom

2. Wrap other end of wire around a thin plastic headband, starting at the point just above your ear. Wrap black electrical tape over that wrapped wire. Put the headband on, and bend the "head mic" into place.

BELT BUCKLE

1. Cut a 2½-by-4½-inch piece of black foam or black construction paper. Use the same decorative technique as used for the cuff (see page 48).

2. Tape a large paper clip to the back of the buckle (same as shoe buckle on page 34) for attaching the buckle to the waist of your jeans.

COCK-A-DOODLE-DOO!

Rule the roost and turn yourself into a feathery fowl!

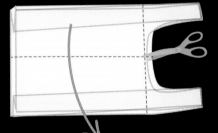

NECK AND WRIST RUFFLES

1. To make the fringed wrist and neck ruffles, flatten a white plastic bag, cut off the handles, and cut in half lengthwise.

2. Use the hole-punch technique from page 5 but run the tape across the width of the bag, 1 inch down from the edge. Run a ribbon through the holes.

masking tape with holes punched through all layers

3. Fringe above and below the tape, fluff, and separate. Trim fringes.

4. Make one for each wrist and combine two for the neck ruff.

MAIN BODY

Gather up a bunch of white plastic bags, and follow the instructions for the fringed popover on page 10.

FEATHERY COMB

Use a red plastic bag and follow the instructions on page 16 to make a feather. To make sure that the comb is super fluffy, cut your feather shape extra wide, with rounded ends. Make the actual feather cuts nice and long. No need to cover the staples with a cardboard strip. Tape the comb to two hair clips.

BEAK

This beak is made from two pieces of yellow Styrofoam from a produce tray, but craft foam will also work. The red wattle is a glued-on strip from a red plastic bag.

FOWL FEET

Stuff a pair of bright yellow rubber gloves with cotton or tissue paper. Tie the stuffed gloves with elastic cord. Fold the cuffs over and double-sided-tape them to the tops of the gloves. Double-sided-tape the bottoms of the palms of the gloves to the tops of your shoes.

YUMMY CUPCAKE

 veryone loves to eat them; now you can actually be one!

1. Cut silver poster board to a desired length and figure out a width that will wrap around you comfortably. You will most likely have to use two pieces taped together, but save the actual taping for later.

2. Make a mark at every *even* number along a straightedge ruler (every 2 inches), the length of the poster board.

3. Flip the poster board over. Make a mark at every *odd* number along a straightedge ruler (every 2 inches), the length of the poster board.

4. Using a yardstick or other straightedge, connect the marks you just made, making a crease in the paper (every 2 inches).

poster board

other side of poster board

6. To hold up the skirt, punch two holes in the front (about 6 to 8 inches apart) and two holes in the back (about 6 to 8 inches apart). From the inside, run a 2-to-3-yard long length of ribbon out through the two front holes. Create suspenders that crisscross in the back, loop the ribbon through the back holes, adjust the suspender length, and tie the ends in a bow.

5. Flip the poster board over and do the same on the opposite side. You will have created 1-inch-wide accordion folds. Use double-sided tape to attach the two pieces of poster board (assuming you needed more than one piece to go around your body).

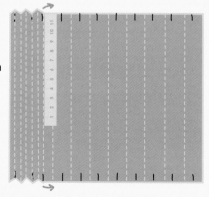

FROSTING HAT

1. Cut a 2-inch-wide strip from the long side of a piece of white poster board to make the headband. We used edging scissors to give it a decorative touch.

2. Knot the closed end of a white kitchen trash bag about a quarter of the way from the bottom. Turn the bag inside out and stuff it with white tissue paper.

3. Line up the open edges of the stuffed bag and tape them closed. Run a piece of double-sided tape along the inside of the headband and only as long as the width of the bag. Tape the bag to the headband. Attach fasteners to the ends of the headband to adjust the fit. Decorate the frosting hat with colored sticker dots for candy sprinkles.

stuffing

double-sided tape

FROSTING RUFFLE

Cut off 6 inches in from the sealed end of a large kitchen garbage bag. Lightly stuff with white tissue paper and seal with double-sided tape. Run a strip of masking tape across the wrong side of the ruffle. To finish the ruffle, use the skirt waist technique on page 6 so the ruffle can be tied comfortably around your neck. Decorate with colored stickers for candy sprinkles.

masking tape with punch holes

bottom end of bag

stuffing

closed with tape

bottom end of bag

FROSTING POUF

Out of what's left of the bag cut two 15-inch squares (or as close to that size as you can manage) of plastic. Tie two ends together tightly. Tuck in a little white tissue stuffing. Tie the other ends, leaving long tails you can attach to your shoelaces or straps. Decorate with colored stickers for candy sprinkles.

53

FROGGY AND PUPPY

Oversize hooded sweatshirts can be the basis for a zoo full of animals. Have a big old brown hoodie? Turn yourself into a bear or a monkey! A gold-colored hoodie would make a perfect lion base, using the cutoff sleeves to make paws for your hands or feet. The possibilities are as unlimited as your imagination. Here are just a few fun creatures.

FROG BODY

1. To make the frog, cut the sleeves from an oversize hooded, green sweatshirt. Save the sleeves for the feet.

2. Put on the sweatshirt, pull on the hood, and draw it tight around your face. Mark two 4½-inch-long lines, positioned 1 inch from the center of the hood and 4 inches from the drawstring edg.

4½-inch-long line

1 inch from center of hood

4 inches from edge of hoodie

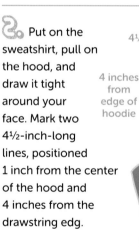

3. When the sweatshirt is off, make a cut along both 4½-inch-long lines

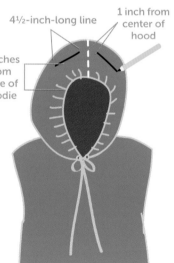

54

4. Put fabric glue on two small Greek-yogurt tubs as shown.

fabric glue in this shape

5. Place the tubs behind the slits. Glue the bottom edge of each tub to the bottom edge of the slit. Let dry. Stretch the top of the slits up and around the tubs in an eyelid shape. Glue and hold in place until the fabric glue begins to dry.

Line glue shape edges up with edges of slit.

6. Let eyeballs dry completely. For eyeball centers, cut out two black circles from felt or construction paper and glue them to the cups.

eyeball

FROGGY FEET

1. Cut down each leftover sleeve to a length a little longer than your foot, heel to toe, including the cuff. Lay each sleeve flat with the seam down. Cut three small triangles out of the wider end and tie the tips of the points together.

2. Cut a 4- to 5-inch-long slit in the seam, starting just above the cuff.

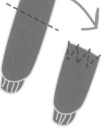

slit on seam

3. Put your foot through the cuff and then out the slit so that the webbed foot flops on top of your shoe. Stick a strip of double-sided tape to the top of each shoe to hold each webbed "foot" in place.

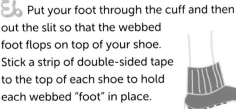

PUPPY BODY

We used a fuzzy-lined hoodie inside out, but any hoodie in a puppy-appropriate color could work. For the ears, just safety-pin a pair of socks onto the hood.

COLLAR

Make a collar using the same technique used for the wrist cuff on page 48. To make the collar long enough, cut two strips of construction paper, 1½ inches wide by 11 inches long. Cut one of the two strips in half and use double-sided tape to add the new pieces to either end of the longer piece. (This way, the seams are on the sides and not right in the middle of the collar.)

DOG BONE COLLAR

Fold a 4-inch square piece of paper in half. Draw half a bone shape and cut it out. Lay it flat and trace it on a piece of silver poster board. Cut it out. Punch a hole in the collar and the tag. Attach the two with a paper clip.

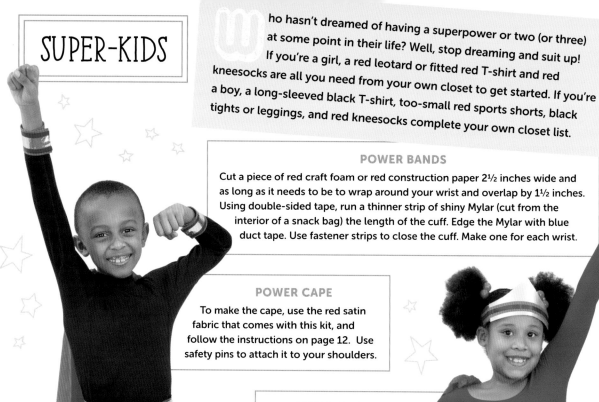

SUPER-KIDS

W ho hasn't dreamed of having a superpower or two (or three) at some point in their life? Well, stop dreaming and suit up! If you're a girl, a red leotard or fitted red T-shirt and red kneesocks are all you need from your own closet to get started. If you're a boy, a long-sleeved black T-shirt, too-small red sports shorts, black tights or leggings, and red kneesocks complete your own closet list.

POWER BANDS

Cut a piece of red craft foam or red construction paper 2½ inches wide and as long as it needs to be to wrap around your wrist and overlap by 1½ inches. Using double-sided tape, run a thinner strip of shiny Mylar (cut from the interior of a snack bag) the length of the cuff. Edge the Mylar with blue duct tape. Use fastener strips to close the cuff. Make one for each wrist.

POWER CAPE

To make the cape, use the red satin fabric that comes with this kit, and follow the instructions on page 12. Use safety pins to attach it to your shoulders.

SUPER CROWN

Draw and cut out a crown-shield shape from silver poster board as shown.

8 inches wide

Cut a strip of leftover skirt fabric long enough to fit around your head. Glue the shield to the center. Attach fastener strips to the ends of the crown so that it fits snugly. Glue a band of red ribbon, red paper, or red craft foam around the crown. Run a stripe of blue duct tape over the red stripe.

SUPER INDOOR SOCK-BOOTS

Run a strip of the blue duct tape that comes with this kit down the front of each red knee sock.

1. Flatten and trim a large recyclable shopping bag (this blue one is from IKEA) to a total width that measures the circumference of your waist plus 24 inches (to accommodate pleats and overlap in the back).

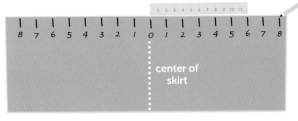

center of skirt

2. Mark the center spot #0 on the wrong side of the skirt strip, and from that center #0, moving to the right and left on either side, mark every 2 inches, giving each mark a number, 1 to 8.

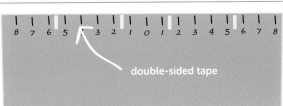

double-sided tape

3. To the right of #0, place double-sided tape between #1 and #2 and #5 and #6. Fold fabric in a vertical line at #3 over to line #1 and stick it down. Congratulations—you've created one pleat. Do it again, vertically folding in line #8 over to line #5. Repeat on the left side.

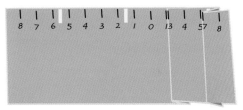

4. To fasten pleats, run a strip of masking tape across the waistband and pleats on the wrong side of the skirt. Run a strip of duct tape across the waist band on the right side of the skirt.

masking tape

5. Hold up skirt and wrap around waist. Use duct tape to close up skirt in the back.

duct tape

SUPER-GIRL BELT

Fold and glue two clean small foil yogurt tops and one large top in the center. Glue in place on the skirt.

can cut down or leave round

SUPER-BOY BELT

Use a strip of blue fabric from the same blue bag, or some other heavy plastic measured to fit comfortably around your waist. Fold and glue two small foil yogurt tops and one large top in the center. Add fastener-strip-closures at the ends.

fastener

57

WILD WEREWOLVES

From your own closet, a black leotard or black fitted T-shirt works for the top, with black bike shorts or leggings for under the skirt. To make the skirt, follow steps 1 and 2 on page 5, but use the gathered ribbon waistband on page 6 instead of the elastic-cord waistband. Finally, slash and shred the hem as dramatically as you like.

ARMS AND LEGS

Cut and shred the ends of a couple of old socks. Different socks will shred differently. There's no perfect way to do this. The final shredded look is what matters. Keep the extra bits for other parts of your costume. Shred another pair for your legs.

Cut off this piece.

CHOKER

The cutoff fingertips from an old furry glove or pom-poms glued to red ribbon make a good choker. Look around for other bits of leftover shredding you can use to make wolfish neckwear.

EARS

Cut craft foam into an ear shape and glue it to a headband. Glue some of the shredded cutoff sock bits to the front and back of the ears. Let dry completely.

glue

sock ends

back view of ears

HANDS

Cut the fingers down on an old pair of gloves. To make nails, accordion-fold a sheet of red cardstock and cut out a nail shape. Glue the nails to the top of the fingers. Let dry completely. Glue furry fabric scraps or more shredded socks around the wrists.

Cut off this piece.

Cut out nail shape.

58

From your own closet, you need a pair of old jeans, and two T-shirts that you don't mind cutting up and painting (one long-sleeved), plus a pair of dark gloves.

FUR CUFFS

Cut two pieces of craft fur, 6 inches by a measurement that fits around your arm plus 2 extra inches. Run fastener strips along the 6-inch edges to close. Wear dark gloves to complete the look.

CLAWED TOP

1. Mark an old T-shirt where you want the claw marks and tears to be. Cut the openings.

Cut out these shapes.

2. Cut the bottom and the sleeves as shown.

fringed sleeves and bottom

3. Put an old long-sleeved T-shirt (white, off-white, or brown: a color similar to your skin color works well) inside the short-sleeved T-shirt, the same way it would be if it were on your body. Draw wounds through the openings with red, pink, and black markers.

Color shapes in through openings.

4. Remove the T-shirt with the wound drawings. Add drips of blood using a red puffy-paint pen.

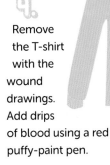

5. Cut holes and tears in an old pair of jeans. Glue little bits of craft fur scraps to the edges of the holes to make it look like fur is coming out of the holes. Add some red paint for drips.

ZOMBIE

T his "costume" is largely about a single special effect...an exceedingly super-duper special effect. Check it out!

BROKEN LEG

THE BONE: Cut open a paper-towel roll the long way, reroll it up tighter, and tape it in place. Tear strips of masking tape the long way. To give the bone texture, completely cover the bone with masking-tape strips. Rub the masking tape with dark shoe polish. Buff off the extra polish.

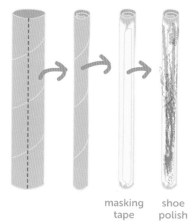

masking tape   shoe polish

THE BLOODY BITS: Cut one end of two toilet-paper rolls in uneven and jagged points. Slather the ends in glue for texture and let dry completely. Paint red and let dry completely.

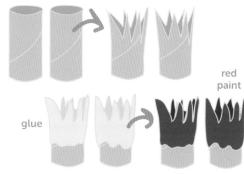

red paint

glue

CONNECT: Glue "bone" to the inside back of the jagged toilet-paper rolls.

sock

Glue "bone" to inside of jagged toilet rolls.

sock

SKIN: Cut a sock (that is close to your own skin tone) in half and fit it over the bloody bits. Glue in place. Add a little red paint to the edges of the socks.

ZOMBIE JEANS: Lay the jeans flat on your work surface and your bone leg on the shin of the jeans just below the knee. With a pen, mark where the tear will be—long enough for some of the bloody bits and skin to show but shorter than the whole thing. Cut the tear. Put the bone inside to see if the opening/tear is the right size.

Cut out tear hole.

FALSE BACK: Cut a scrap of denim from another pair of jeans to the width of your zombie jean leg and a little longer than the whole fake bone plus bloody bits. Glue the bone plus bloody bits to the wrong side of the denim and let it dry completely. Slip the whole thing (fabric patch with glued-on bone) up into the pant leg and position it behind the tear. Glue the edges of this "patch" all around to the inside front edges of the tear with fabric glue. Let dry completely.

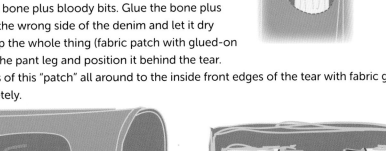

Glue all around patch (after gluing down bone pieces).

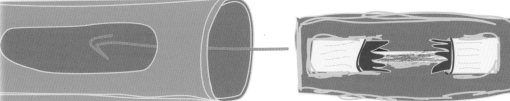

THE REST
To finish off this zombie, wear an old grubby T-shirt under an old torn-up flannel shirt. Greenish makeup is a nice touch.

ROBOT

One part Tin Man, one part jack-in-the-box, this costume is as much fun to make as it is to run around in.

BODY

1. Find a rectangular carton that will cover most of your body to your knees once you climb inside and poke your head out (see photo).

2. Remove any short flaps and tape any open long flaps.

Tape closed.

Cut off short flaps.

3. Stand carton on one short end. Using a craft knife, cut out the bottom of the box. (NOTE: You must ask a grown-up to do this for you.)

Cut out bottom.

4. In the center of the other short end, trace a circle with a diameter large enough for your head to fit through. We use a pan lid $7^{1}/_{4}$ inches in diameter. Use a craft knife to cut out the circle, as well as 5-inch-wide-by-7-inch-long armholes on each side of the box.

5. Try on the box to make sure your head and arms fit through comfortably. Make whatever small adjustments you need to make.

6. Paint the entire carton silver. Decorate with cutout circles, lids, an old calculator, bottle caps, stickers, quarter-machine domes, etc. Let your imagination go wild.

ARMS AND HANDS

Make Bubble Wrap cuffs for forearms and upper arms using the same method as for the space cuffs (see page 44). Silver ski gloves make excellent robot hands.

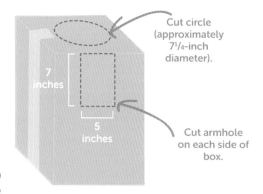

Cut circle (approximately $7^{1}/_{4}$-inch diameter).

7 inches

5 inches

Cut armhole on each side of box.

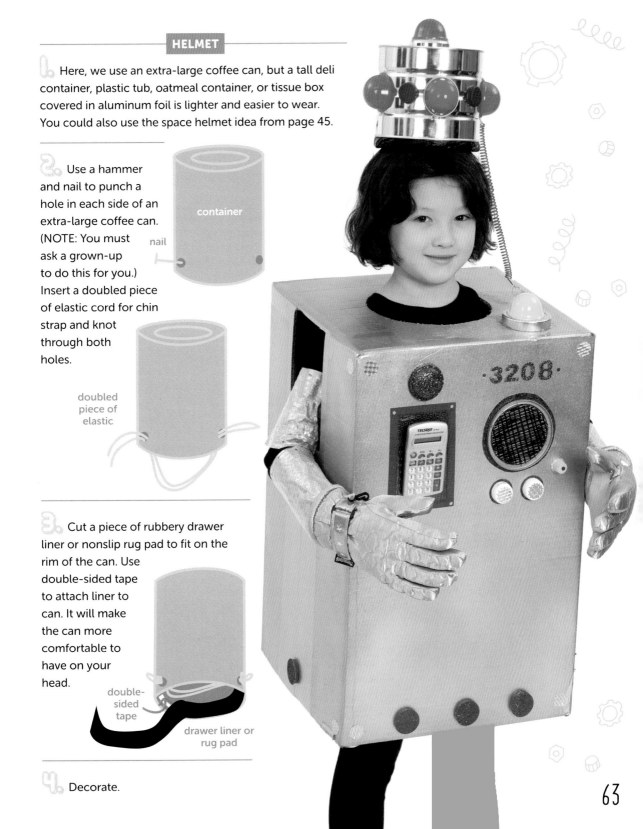

HELMET

1. Here, we use an extra-large coffee can, but a tall deli container, plastic tub, oatmeal container, or tissue box covered in aluminum foil is lighter and easier to wear. You could also use the space helmet idea from page 45.

2. Use a hammer and nail to punch a hole in each side of an extra-large coffee can. (NOTE: You must ask a grown-up to do this for you.) Insert a doubled piece of elastic cord for chin strap and knot through both holes.

container

nail

doubled piece of elastic

3. Cut a piece of rubbery drawer liner or nonslip rug pad to fit on the rim of the can. Use double-sided tape to attach liner to can. It will make the can more comfortable to have on your head.

double-sided tape

drawer liner or rug pad

4. Decorate.

KOOKY CLOWN

ou don't need a costume to think about joining the circus—but it could come in handy. Of all the costumes, clown wear is easiest to scrounge from your closet. It's all about exaggerated sizes—too small, too big, etc. Our top is a too-small knit dress in a clown-perfect print. Plopped over colorful leggings, colorful boots, with a hat/wig, our clown garb is halfway home.

CLOWNIFY TOPS AND BOTTOMS

Open a small hole in the dress hem and run a length of craft wire all the way through the hem's tunnel, wrapping the ends together when they meet. (Tip: Tape the end of the wire and it will snake through without snagging.) You could use this same technique with the pant hems or the waistband of super-baggy adult-size pants. (Tip: If you wire the waistband, you will need clip-on suspenders to hold up your pants.)

HAT/WIG

Make T-shirt hair following the instructions on page 15. Attach the hem of the T-shirt hair to the inside of the hat using double-sided tape or glue. Make several largeish flowers, following the instructions on page 16. Use brad fasteners for the flower's centers to hold the petals together and to secure the flowers to the hat.

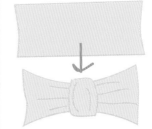

hat

glue

T-shirt wig piece

BOW AND FLOWER

Make a big silly bow by cutting a section of a plastic gift bag, gathering it in the center, and covering the center with another strip of the bag.

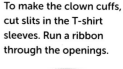

COLLAR

Make a fun collar by cutting up an old, colorful T-shirt as shown.

CUFFS

To make the clown cuffs, cut slits in the T-shirt sleeves. Run a ribbon through the openings.